Contents

This book is dedicated to our mum, Jane Booth.

The Boothies
(She Laughed More Than She Cried)

What's in a name - Abbreviations

Waste ground	Oller
Bombdie	Bombed out house, derelict
Bung up	Lift up
Fade	Rotten fruit
Barra or Barrow	Handcart
Dixie	Keep watch
Rossi	Roscommon Street School
Greaty	Great Homer Street
Neddy	Netherfield Road
Scotty	Scotland Road
The Bagot	John Bagot Hospital
Loosie	Single cigarette
Entry, back jigger	Alleyway
Oilcloth	Linoleum

All in scouse dialect

Preface

It all began on 7th May 1948 when 'Yours Truly' was born, the first child, a boy, to William Henry Booth and Jane Booth nee Warburton.

They never realised what they were letting themselves in for - in the best possible way, of course.

My mother and father were not rich and I was born in a cellar at the top of Gordon Street, not ideal conditions to come into the world. After leaving Mill Road Maternity Hospital, my mother was 20 years of age and my father about 22. They were young and in love and nothing else matters.

They had a large family to count on and they were well cared for by both families.

Imagine those days, the cellars were damp, dark and infected by all manner of vermin. That's where it all began. The journey starts here at the top of Gordy.

I come from a very large family with a real story to tell. Stay with me and have a laugh.

Bill (10), Alan (9), Ray (8), John (7)

Chapter 1 – The Tribe

Soon after I was born, well, months to be precise, my mother was again pregnant and on 10th May 1949 another boy arrived, my brother, John. One year and three days after me. My mam had just turned 21 and had two boys under 13 months.

Living in a cellar at the top of Gordy was not ideal but they got on with life. I wonder how they coped but in those early days they had little choice.

My dad had various jobs, all casual. He wasn't always working so they obviously struggled to bring us up. They were only young. From now on it gets harder. The inevitable happened one year after John, boy number three arrived on cue. Our Alan, my mam would have known, was huge and still is. The gentle giant arrived on the scene and now they have three sons, one year each apart.

What's going on? They must have been gluttons for punishment or there was a reason for all these "Boothies" arriving so regular. Well, who knows, being only three at the time.

But it's beginning to unfold, son by son, brother by brother. Circumstances were looking better for our parents. My mother's mum, our nan, was living at the bottom end of Gordon Street at number 40, and she was offered somewhere else to live, with a job thrown in. Happy days. My mam and dad were moving down the street to number 40 to the ancestral home, no removal van required. The handcart served its purpose. Great! My parents had a real house. Two up two down, back yard. It was the business. It was clean when my nan left, it was spotless after my mam had finished with it.

My nan was a workaholic, she never tired. She brought up seven kids on her own. My grandad died young, at aged 38 I believe. What a woman, I follow her, all in the genes. You will read the word genes many times before the epilogue.

My mother at 18 years old. Eat your heart out Elizabeth Taylor!

Number 40 Gordon Street was our life in those days. It's everything I remember about my youth, about my parents' trials and tribulations. It was a very happy house with my mam and dad, singing day and night, children laughing and crying. It was a busy life to juggle, this and that, but they succeeded to improve their life.

Then when all was going to plan, guess what, along comes another Boothie. Yes, you have it spot on, another boy/brother, more or less 12 months apart.

Four boys in four years, and all without Viagra. What an achievement.

No wonder my dad could hold his drink, he must have only had time to come up for breath. Before he was wetting another son's head, that's Bill, John, Alan, Ray (it was written!).

It was all starting to get a bit crowded with six under one roof at 40 Gordy. Where did we all sit in that small house, I don't know? I don't remember but they thrived and things got better. My parents had four boys, back to back. It was hard going but my parents were proud and my dad must have been on free ale for weeks.

The days went by and all was fine. John as a baby would pinch my bottle, that Alan would pinch Ray's, and we were complete, so we thought. Not likely! My dad had other ideas.

Five years later, yes you have it spot on, along came Wayne, another son and brother number five. Yes, the five-card trick!

What an achievement. My mother must have been exhausted. Not only had she had five boys, but she had them all before she was thirty years of age. I mean come on, five boys (Boothies), that's a tribe. Be scared – look out Gordy - we have arrived. God bless mam and dad.

This was about the time the "Four Just Boys" (not Wayne, he came five years after Bill) had started to gain their entrepreneurial talents. I remember the oldest of Enid Blyton's Famous Five was only nine, the youngest one would set off on a journey. That would have people saying, like, but they're only kids, how can they do that? Where do they get the time? Where do they get the energy? Where do they get the brains?

You have guessed it, the boss, William Henry Booth Snr and Jane Booth, the mix was set, then we were formed, and finally the mould was broken. These four lads shook the world (and Greaty) before the Beatles were heard of.

With five lads to look after, all under nine years old, that must have took some doing. Mind you it was nothing. I have heard some people having ten and even 12 kids. Come on, that is a tribe!

But I am sure most people who had lots of children were around the 30s, 40s, 50s before my mam and dad's day. Big families were the norm in those days. The saying goes they brought each other up. A very true saying, they looked after their own.

My parents' lives must have been very full. Where the money came from, God knows. I was too young. My nanny Kate was a great help.

Aunties and uncles alike all pulled together. In those days they had to, it was well documented.

I was given a title by my dad. I was 'No 1 Son'. He always referred to me as that. And yes, I have to say I had his ways. Not half!

Anyway, 12 months after Wayne the inevitable happened. My mother had a baby girl at home in 40 Gordon Street. My dad was drunk for a month. Her name was Gail and it was written.

A girl for my mam to look after her. Anyway, the tribe is all complete. Another chapter begins, me the oldest, Gail the youngest. Family life has changed forever.

Chapter 2 – Streets ahead of the Rest

Back in the late 50s/early 60s every street had a 'Del Boy'. Every six houses had a budding 'Mr Fix It' and every other street had a future millionaire. But no-one had what we had. And that was four of them. Our Wayne was too young yet. In every one of us at that time, you could see if you looked closely enough.

The Richard Branson, the Kevin Keegan, the Alfie Packenham of this world. Starting to find their feet already, to shake the world. Well, we will start with Greaty first.

The first steps were made when I was nine/ten. We sort of stumbled upon the idea by chance while we were stripping a bombdie from head to toe, or roof to cellar if you like. When you pull up the floorboards you can strip the copper wire from within. What do you do with all the floorboards? When you take the door of its hinges, after taking off the brass handles, what do you do with the door? While you're stripping the windows of its cast iron weights, what do you do with the window frames? All together lads, chop it up and sell it!

We have arrived on a doorstep near you very soon will hear that knock on the door from one of the four choir boys repeating those now famous words, "Any wood missus?".

"Go on, Mrs King, Mrs Smith, Mrs Kinney … it's freezing, we want to go home."

It worked every time. We were made for it.

The customers were smitten. From that day on we would use every trick in the book, invented by ourselves, to get a sale. And each day we would learn from the day before. We had a great arsenal and each one of us had an art that they tweaked to perfection.

Starting with our Ray, and working down, if I put 13 bundles of wood in his arms and said, "Follow me", we would then knock on someone's door and say, "Any wood, missus".

"Not tonight, son, we have plenty."

"Okay, but it's the last, we just have to get rid of this, and our Ray can go home to bed."

She would take one look at him, six years old, freezing to death, about two foot six.

"Ah go on then, but not tomorrow, okay."

"All right, missus"

Another one chalked up for the Boothies. Before child labour was frowned upon now that six-year-old has been and done the lot, and has just booked his moon voyage with Richard Branson, because he has done everything down here. Only kidding.

They key to it all is catch them young. I'm sure he learnt a lot from those days. He was certainly self-taught. From one street to another, in the depths of winter, to get shut of 13 bundles of wood, our entire worth for a full night's work would be no more than 1 shilling and threepence. Four of us, for four hours work, for one and three. In today's money it equals seven pence. Come on, get on that, that is child labour. So what, he loves it. In for a penny, in for a pound. It was all about the knowledge, all about the journey for the Boothies.

While we were selling firewood, we would keep our eyes and ears open for the pearl in the oyster, the jewel in the crown, or, in our case, the golden nugget, for the week.

If it was something given, something we found in one of the bombdies, or something in a bin, we always came up lucky. A silver cross pram, an antique clock, an item of jewellery lost, we scanned everything. Remember it was dog eat dog. Everyone was at it, no-one had money. If you wanted something you had to duck and dive, no-one gave you anything. It was better than going to uni, but without degrees.

Our playing field, or the area we visited every day, stretched from the end of Greaty to the other end. That was our daily ritual. In the summer we went further afield, into the unknown or another man's land. That's how hungry and devious we were. Remember, we were then 11 down to seven, not the Four Just Men, but the Boothies. That was enough to put people on their guard.

If we were up and out, and especially thirst thing, there was a reason. Some of my brothers would be doing a paper round, our Alan worked on Neddy Road for Bill Moneypenny. Alan loved it and they loved him. He was a grafter. Me and John would help the milkman. Why? Because that's what the Boothies did. They used their guile and energy pursuing all manner of entrepreneurial deeds, purely for gain of course, what else?

We found that if you were up early and already focussed on the catch, then you have that head start and I can tell you it came naturally. It was in the genes. My dad was the master and the students took it all in. We were born too soon for celebrity status. Lord Sugar's loss!

You had to be able to stop what you were doing and gather the prize. If we were playing football anywhere, it might not be in our street or area, if something came up and you could see it was going to be an earner, then everything was put on hold. We could be miles away.

If we saw a family in the process of leaving their house to move to another, we would stay close and scan what was happening. The minute the removal van left we would be over the back wall. We would check out the yard, then take a look through the windows to see if everywhere looked empty. Then we would leave. The next day we would be observing, keeping close was the key.

Once we established the house was empty after two or three days, we would make our move. We would never take anything from a house unless we knew they had left and were not coming back. In those days people left on a regular basis, to move up market areas they thought at the time, like Speke, Kirby, Walton, etc. Most settled, stayed and brought up their families, some tried to move back, but it was no good. People were leaving. Areas torn apart, so sad.

If we had an opportunity gain access to an empty house, vacated – this was not a bombdie. A bombdie only got in a not liveable state because it would have been bombed during the Blitz and left that way. But remember the war finished in 1945 and I never came on the scene until 1948 and it was a good eight or nine years before I acquired the knowledge. So those bombdies could have been in that state from any time from 1940 up to I was eight or nine. So, we're talking 1956 onwards. Now that is a long time for a bombdie not to have been excavated or was it just there was no-one around with the nose and brain at the time. Probably it was just waiting for the ultimate magpies to come along. Enter the Boothies.

Our aim when entering a bombdie or empty house would be to strip it from top to bottom. And I mean bottom, cellar and all. Rats never bothered us. The roof first for any lead flashing, aluminium aerials, scrap downspouts, toilet cisterns, lead pipes, copper ball. All windows sash cast iron weights, all external and internal brass door handles, any lead in kitchen, copper wash boilers, cooker waste pipes.

Once we had achieved the basic strip we would start upstairs, all the floorboards would come up before stripping all of the copper wire from the floor and ceiling, space, electrics would be killed from the cupboards in case they were live. Every door would come off its hinges. The outside door would also be stripped. The toilet seats would go. Any scrap that had been accumulated would go into the back yard ready for removal. While two of us systematically took the house to skeleton proportions.

The other two would start to move the booty pram-load-by-pram-load. If no pram, then by steering the cart. It could take hours. Remember, we are 11, 10, 9 and 8 in age but clued up as the haul was being moved to 40 Gordon Street.

As me and John were the oldest, then we decided what was to be moved first and obviously it was the items that had more value, less bulky and less noticeable. So, the pram first would be filled with metal, for example, copper, brass, lead, aluminium, any antiques that could be sold quickly.

Me and John would carry on stripping the carcass and meticulously stacking and stowing everything in regimental order. Doors that could be sold whole, toilet seats paint and resell, mirrors, furniture, rags, copper wire bagged, floorboards would go back to 40 Gordon Street to recycle into firewood. Everything was now ready after removal to separated, with the job complete a process that would have taken a maximum of one day.

Early start, late finish, the Boothies, we never looked at the clock. To this day I don't think any of us actually wears a watch. Why no matter what you do with your day it all brings five o'clock, a true saying of my dad's.

Once we had took stock, and only one day to complete, that's how quick and dedicated we were to the task. No-one could come near us. We were that motivated. There is no better feeling than being one step ahead of the rest. Mostly while the rest were still in bed or playing football in the street.

It was as if you like, you could say, an army of ants moving stuff 10 times bigger than themselves. If a door was 6ft, a floor board 10ft, a bag of copper wire half a hundredweight, none of those efforts bothered us. No obstacle was immovable. No fireplace too heavy to rip out from the wall. We had the lot: brains, strength, energy. No other four entrepreneurs were in our age group. Look out world, the Boothies are coming.

These were our bombdies. No-one ever worried about getting dirty. Down with the old and up with the new (that never stayed long). In the background is the Royal Hospital back in the day.

Once we have moved everything to 40 Gordy, we would take time to plan this out on. Nothing moved for days.

It had to be all sorted out bundled, wrapped, presentable added to and so on ready for the sell. In the meantime, we carried on with our full-time career, selling firewood. Each night, year in year out, we had hundreds of customers. All signed up to the Booth motto 'if in doubt shout the Boothies, there will be one near you who will hear'.

Mostly our local scrap metal dealer at the bottom of our street, Mr. Packenham, or Paki as we knew him, he was Jewish and very shrewd. He would send his own men up the entry if it was a big haul and it was mostly what he did. We would save it, store it, add to it, but you have to be careful. Every other potential entrepreneur would know we had just done our kill and if your back door was not locked up it would go.

There was a lot of kids doing what we did but not on a business scale like us. Mostly what we would call part time they either never have the energy or the brains or they never needed to. If their dad had a good job, they always got their pocket money but not us though, if my dad was not working we got nothing. This isn't very good where would we get our treats from.

How could we go to the pictures and all those things kids do with money? Not only was there other kids trying to pinch your booty, but the rag man, or tatter as we call them, would come down every day shouting "scrap iron, any old scrap iron". My dad would also be shouting those same words and doing very different entries around Anfield and Goodison but we will leave that to later on.

Now as we approached Saturday morning Packi would close half day. So, we were up and ready for the mass exodus. Normally my dad would have clocked what we had and he would have had it worked out to the penny. It was an Aladdin's cave of joy. Off we went with his Barrow down the entry, it would be Rod Starkey, a mate of my dad's, who was also a tatter but worked for Packi on Saturday morning.

One of the Boothies would be in Packi's when the stuff arrived. There could be 20 barrow loads, that's without the rags, jam jars, and light metal which we carried ourselves, all removed from 40 Gordy. We would all attend the big weigh in. All the metal was weighed first in the back warehouse where all the gold was kept. I mean brass, copper, lead, aluminium, all neatly locked away. Then came the light iron, lastly the jam jars, hundreds of them. Packi would then go into his office, my dad was there and my dad had a brain like a computer, he never needed a calculator. He had it worked out before Packi. Anyway, when I got paid out guess who ended up with more money than us four? Yep you're right, my mam and dad in that order, weighed in.

We were paid on one occasion for the full weight in £18 2s 4p. It was a virtual treasure trove to us kids in those days. The equivalent of one month's wages for the average man. Even if my dad was working, which he was not at the time, he was only going out with the barrow. We had to muck in. My mum got £6, dad got £4, and we got £2 each. To us it was the culmination of a full week's work of stripping, moving, sorting, and getting rid of. It would work out in today's terms at 40 pence a day for 5 days. Real raft, come on, honestly, can you see today's Fauntleroy's doing that? 'No, it's cold out mam', mind you £2 each in those days was worth twenty times more than today. The Boothies came through again. Weighed in.

After all that was over. and it was only one incident in a thousand, in those days we went back to an empty yard, ready to chop, bundle and get everything ready for the coming Monday evening. We would be ready when we returned from school to go out with the wood. A dozen bundles in John's arms, a dozen in Alan's and six in Ray's. Remember he was still only a baby, but a sleeping giant, waiting to use all that skill he learned on them cold nights down Greaty, priceless.

Once on the streets I would direct them to the customers, who to go to, and who to leave that night. We would again as always be vigilant while delivering the wood. No stone must be left unturned. If we spotted anything an aluminium kettle, a jam jar, a piece of wood, any empty bottles, anything, must be picked up and brought back to 40 Gordy. It's called little acorns. Never get complacent you start with one item and end up with a thousand quickly.

We never rested on our laurels. Time was money and never the Twain shall meet. We were ruthless, more ruthless than we are now. Why, because if we never met those challenges how would it have changed us. I might have been a bank clerk or worked in an office, no need to get your hands dirty or even say I am cold. No, it was there, we done it, it shapes us, and to this day it has never left us. It's in the genes. And I for one would not have anyone say otherwise. Today we can laugh, but not then. It was serious. It's in us all. There was no-one who could strip a length of copper wire faster than our John. Wicked.

Thank God health and safety and political correctness came sixty years after these boys playing out.

Chapter 3 - All for one and one for all

As four brothers I think we got on quite well. I was always very vocal, always giving orders, I mean I was only 12 or 13 years of age. I felt I knew more; the brain was working overtime to take things in and get things done. Our Alan and John called me everything and you know they were right. I was a slave driver but it always worked in our favour. Our Ray was younger but we all did our bit. My mum I am sure in those days took no sides. We only had one goal - making money.

As kids I fear we were into everything but you only went so far, you never cross the line. If we did, we had our mam to contend with and she was ruthless. She had to be with five lads, Gayle was still a baby.

I would have my dad any day. My dad was more vocal and he knew what to call you which hurt. I got called "you girl, you dope". You name it we got it, verbally of course. While my mum had a wicked right hand. Just like mine, if she caught you your head would be sore for days. She was strong like my nan. And if that never worked there was always those forever words "get to bed, get up and stay there".

In those days when we were sent to bed it was like Colditz only colder. All there was in the room with a bed, a window to look out of, no views, no grass, no sandy beaches, just Ben Jones's back yard and his pigeon loft. Oh, maybe a cat or two on the back-entry wall.

The bedroom never had all today's mod-cons. Today if your mum said go to bed you thought, yes, a bit of peace, I will put on the telly, turn the central heating up, play on my computer, contact my mates on Facebook. It's better than a week in Benidorm but without the sun. You don't know you are born with a nice cosy bed all your own. Not four in a small single bed. The words "bringing us closer together" was an understatement.

Can you imagine in winter, 7-8 o'clock, four of us sent to bed and the room was freezing? The windows were full of ice – on the inside! We had only Napoleon's coat to keep four of us warm, an army blanket and my dad's winter overcoat. Bloody hell – someone hurry up and invent central heating.

There was two of us one end in bed and two the other end. We had a gob full of feet.

John (10), Ray (7), Gail (1), Bill (11), Alan (9), Wayne (2)
The four eldest kids who shook Greaty.

We knew every spider by name and every insect or mouse that found its way under the floorboards. But I do remember had a dartboard, rubber darts, the sucker type.

The summers were great in those days. When you got sent to bed you could open the window, climb out onto the back-kitchen roof, or the outside bog roof, and get a tan. If you got caught you got battered. I'm sure all four of us would have spent a few nights looking out of the window, the insects would have been all we had for company.

In the summer we still sold firewood, mostly to older people who still got cold in the summer nights in those little back to back houses. But you know what, when we walked into those houses carrying the wood, you went into their parlour or living room and they were cosy and warm with the coal fire burning away, and the wood we provided at a small price.

We felt good but do you know those old people with shawls around them weren't old. They just looked old with the day in day out routine, no weekends off, no trips out to the countryside, no seven days in Benidorm, not much to look forward to. Work and the same four walls.

But in the summer, they would be sitting on their immaculate steps outside, or playing rounders with the kids, skipping and playing cricket and football, keeping an eye on their kids playing out. Not like today. They have one hand on the pram and the other on the mobile texting – another safe invention.

My parents had some great nights in our house. We would all creep downstairs and peep into the room. They have all come back from the pub. My dad was a real singer, no-one touched him, not even my Uncle Robbie, my dad's brother. They were always at each other. My mam could sing too, but when my dad sang, everyone shut up. Eventually we all ended up in the room once they were pissed.

We knew we were okay to join in. My dad would bring crisps, nuts and lemonade home from the pub for us all. He was very thoughtful. My mam would dance and sing, she was always happy. They never had much, but they were well liked and they always had friends. My dad could sing and my mam would laugh and smile. They had it all.

On New Year's Eve we had a big party. The table was full of all sorts. My mam and dad would go to the pub, then people could come to ours. We would go out to their house at 12 o'clock we all went outside. Everyone sang Aulde Lang Syne and everyone kissed strangers.

I kept looking for Ann Hughes. I had a childhood crush on her. Everyone had a great time, all in the same boat, no-one with money, not a car in the street. We had two handcarts. They were great days, or is it because we were young and carefree? Those three little words sums up our days down Greaty. Not just the four of us, but Wayne and Gail were toddlers now. I loved those days. If I had a Jaguar, I would give it up easily to be ack there then for a bit longer young and carefree. Cathy and the kids would eventually be here to look forward to later on, once I had grown up.

We never had many mishaps when we were young. Apart from our Alan getting rheumatic fever when he was young. Now and again one of us would fall into a bombdie cellar, or myself would try to escape from the Police through a fanlight window, only to cut my leg open. A few of us would fall off the back-yard wall while running the walls or billy banding from each side.

But all in all, no major mishaps when we were kids. God knows how we never had. I do remember many a time mam running up Newsham Street with one of us teaming with blood, to get the bus on Scotland Road to

Stanley Hospital. I would like a penny for every time that happened. No one had a car in the street and we couldn't afford taxis and never had a phone. Can you imagine today's women doing that with six kids? Washing their clothes by hand, no hoovers, no Sky TV, no mobile phones, no fast food. They don't build women like they used to.

As kids we played a lot of football not only in the street but in Shaw Street Park and other areas. We played on the tarmac on Neddy Road. We had a great team, most of my brothers were good. John was great with his head. He was only small but what a player. He was also hard. He never cared how big you were, he never backed down. He was like a Rottweiler at your feet.

Our Alan was a great centre half who could also play in the middle. You never crossed Alan. He would be looking for you the whole game. There was only ever going to be one winner, he never took prisoners. Next stop Stanley Hospital. Dedicated to make you hurt but fair.

As kids we played street matches but not all our games were at home. Others could be played at City Road, behind Everton's ground. We would play against a mate of mine's team. I worked at Venmores with him. We played over Scotland Road at Gerard Gardens, Portland Gardens, Tommy Whites Gardens, Islington. We would travel by foot remember, no mountain bikes back then, and team coaches had not been invented then. We would walk for miles, we were fit. We could literally play all day, no 45 minutes each way, that's for Spice Boys. We would play first to 20 goals. It could take hours and after the game we would walk home, normally in the dark and starving.

Imagine the Premier League players. They have just played four hours, oxygen in the dressing rooms. Ambulances in the car park. And then having to walk or get the bus home. Com on – in your dreams, or nightmares. Celebrities.

My mam always said, "don't go far, are you listening?". "Yes mam!"

We would go about 8 o'clock and not get back to 8 at night, sometimes without any food. We could have gone on a bike ride to Crosby. The bikes could have died on the way. Each bike was made by our resident engineer, Franny Lownes. Have bike will travel. Supply your own brakes and saddle. We had the des res bikes, their life expectancy which was nil which is Packi's, sorry can't see no lights.

The bikes were advertised locally as the here today gone soon form of transport. But we managed to get to all the exotic places, like Aigburth, Bootle, Crosby, New Brighton, Wally Hall park and Fazakerly. These childhood dreams. The true meaning of the word vision. Nothing was impossible in those days. As brothers we stuck together and the world was our oyster. And other teams would say 'We are playing the Boothies, fame at last!'.

As I have mentioned in passing we never had a lot of free time. They were mostly the summer days being longer, and why would you want to stay in the house looking at four walls. We were not rich we had no bling bling. We survived on our wits. And we had that in abundance. No-one of our age group came near to us. We explored and exploited anything that moved during our daily or nightly wood delivery round. We would introduce new perks to our customers. We were always polite that was the key to our success and longevity in the wood processing industry.

We prided ourselves on a 24/7 delivery service. We would be available any time, summer or winter. We were available to run errands. We say messages. We would take away any unwanted items, examples waste paper, jam jars, lemonade and milk bottles, cardboard, any old cans etc, all to be sold on of course. We were steadily becoming a collection point, while delivering the wood, any paper collected would be bundled and delivered to any of a dozen chippies. They were all on our books. What better way to eat your fish and chips with a picture and story off the Boothies. Wanted dead or live. Only kidding. They wish.

A very lucrative endeavour that was purposely drilled into each one of us when we left our business premises at 40 Gordy. And my motto to the brothers was don't come back empty handed. It was a gift most 8, 9, 10- and 11-year olds never had, but we did, and no one gets one over the Boothies. They wrote the rules.

At that point in our lives the brain matter was working overtime. Trying to come up with new ways of making money. Remember what we earned two thirds went to our mam. I am not joking, we were really little angels but we got up to all kinds.

We would do a favour for anyone. We were brought up to be police, especially to our elders. Everyone knew the Boothies, we used to get a lot of compliments. My mam had us well cleaned and turned out.

Especially Sunday. I think I was about 13 when I would get the morning paper, mostly Sundays, I would always look in the racing page. Anyway, those days you had to get someone to put your bets on.

The bookies had just started to open and I thought I was Peter O'Sullivan, Gym Crack. I started doing a 5p Yankee. I'd get the paper the next day to see if I had won. You had to get the winners. Anyway, it went on for years, getting coppers back, until one day, I had three times six pence doubles and a six pence treble, two shillings in those days. All three won. I can still remember their names: Ragusa, Ragotto, Rappani. Three Irish horses, they are imprinted in my brain. And so is the man who went to collect my winnings. It's a good job I was not half with my mate Jimmy Maddox. I sued to have a bet with, he would have hung me from a bombdie cellar.

My dad of all people done a runner. Him and Georgie Connor his mate at the time, or should I say drinking partner. Three winners a virtual treasure trove, gone until returns.

I said, 'Dad I have got three winners up, it took years to get that bet up'.

'Don't worry lad, I will get it for you.'

Eight o'clock that night my mam said I wonder where he is. I said who, she says, your dad. Wait till I get him. I have an idea, you see mam, I won a few bob which I have not seen. I gave the ticket to my dad.

'You what, ah, you thick dope', it was a word I was often called where money was concerned.

I thought he would come back, you don't know your dad. Get down that Bents House at the bottom of Rossi and see if he is there and go the back way.

Okay mam.

Mam, he's here. Well not quite. He is trying to get here he's bouncing off every wall in the entry.

Wait till I get him in here. It's alright mam, I don't mind him having a few bob.

I'll a few bob yeh, get to bed.

Ah hey mam.

My dad eventually sobered up after falling over a few times. It was funny. The money never mattered but I did get some change. Life goes on. I would be 19 before I got that bet up again. How time flies. I never did ask my dad how much I got back off the bet. No, I will rephrase that. How much did you get back, you learn from all those people and take it with you on a journey. We had some laughs.

On the way to school each morning we would go by way of the entries in case we could find something. We would drop all the bins and look inside. The bins weighed a ton. We were only babies but we could life them, no John Lewis gyms for us, all man-made stuff. Then we passed a few hand carts that were parked up. We would lift the canvass and low and behold mega, apples, oranges, bananas, etc, grab – and away. We could not take into school, back home, put them upstairs, back to school late, monitor report. To head after assembly, why were you late boys. Sorry sir, forgot my dinner money. So, you all forgot your dinner money? All three of you? Liars – hand out.

Yes Sir, oh no where's my hand. Don't let that happen again, not bloody likely. Then came John, then Alan.

No daytime telly for the Boothies when we were young. We were never allowed to stay in bed. We were told from babies, time is money. We never wasted time and never wasted money. We were up before the milkman. No need to stay in bed, the computer was a long way off, so our forte was our energy, our choir boy looks and our cheek, we had the lot.

We were streets ahead of all the other kids, purely because there was four of us, soon to become five. To be honest, you could not live with that, we had the lots, brains, energy enthusiasm and most of all, great genes passed down by two good-looking hard-working parents.

We couldn't go wrong and we milked every opportunity we got. We never turned anything down. The old in for a penny in for a pound. Our motto, little acorns. Never a word said in jest. As the older brother and boss, I knew each of our strengths and of course weaknesses, the latter were few and far between.

Why because we were Boothies. The Boothies always came through. Not many lived with us. We were clued up from five in the morning till ten at night, then ready for the next day. I have always said, if you're going to do something, do it right and you can go back, get it wrong and you have lost a customer.

When you are 8 to 10 years old every day was an adventure, something new around. I have to say that the time we had as kids, those entrepreneurial traits. The kicks we got with the sting. Looking for the next quest, we done more up to our 15th years of age than some people ever do in a lifetime. Today it's all about how much benefits you can get without going out the door.

They go to their grave with credits that you can fit on a lucky 15 betting slip. What a waste. No adventures, no energy, just waiting to die. But not the Boothies.

I remember once, and I mean once, we all had to watch thunder and lightning till it went off. It was the only form of weather that stopped us from doing our daily tasks. Not snow, not rain, not wind, not cold, nor heat, the Boothies were hardy.

Now and again those winter nights in the late 50s/early 60s were raw cold and they would bite through you. Remember we were babies, aged 10 downwards. Today 8-10-year olds can't be separated from their phone for more than five minutes. No imagination needed, boring and repetitive.

In those hot summer days, we would look for anything that could fill our day. Not many people bought firewood in the summer, only the elders.

So, we would arrange football matches anywhere. We would walk all day to play. There was the Jimmy Melia Award Scheme at Shaw Street Park. We would also sit on Maggie Jane's shed and play cards but you needed money for that. We would dip the bins for milk bottles, lemo bottles, jam jars, rag, metal, anything we could sell, you know it was better than sitting on your arse waiting to turn sixty so you can sit on your arse. Not the Boothies, that's for old and dead people. We wanted to explore, investigate, travel, compete, we were alive and we needed challenges. Every day we had to stay alert. Test the brain and body.

I think even today if we were born into this modern age we would be the same. Its about what you inherit. Look, if your parents have all the I am alive qualities, then we are going to inherit them traits. We're not going to make for the nearest couch or sofa and sit down talking, texting and using social media about what other people are doing with their day, their lives. Who cares? Come on, that's for old men and old women. You make your own life and you keep your own counsel and you can't go wrong.

So even in today's society we would adapt to whatever and still be using the old brain matter instead of letting Google sort it for us. I mean we're the Boothies and the Boothies don't delegate, they do it themselves.

Can you imagine today's social media, Google, mobile phones, lap tops, tablets, etc. Just to have a mobile phone each and to be able to send a picture to any of us would have been magic. I am sure with the help of today's technology we would have cleaned up. Imagine, five little millionaires before we had left school. Come on anything that was worth selling was sold.

With all those gadgets we could have sourced areas to check out, barter online, eBay, you name it, if you have the energy, the knowledge to buy and sell, the work rate you are going to succeed. If the Boothies had an easier way to go about their business they would have done it.

I don't know we preferred to get our hands dirty. We are still like that today. Would we if we could afford to get kitted out with Apple mobiles? I doubt it. Our Ray would have been good at it, he was very studious. The rest of us would prefer the hands-on approach, especially with our older customers. Remember the more help care wide you gave the more you would collect at Christmas. I know it's not nice to think like that but when you have nothing and work hard all year so them few extra shilling each is a bonus to us. And a thank you from our year long customers we would get Christmas boxes from a selection of people. We have been employed by if you like, the scrap dealer, the chippies, the customers. It was all gratefully received with thanks.

I look back today and wonder, was our childhood wasted, did we miss out on other things, did we have tunnel vision and have only one object in mind: money? Could we have expended our education? Could we have learnt new skills? Could we have been more academic? Could we have used that time better? Well, the answer is no. Why? Because them days everyone was in the same boat. Yes, money was a motivation. Everyone needed extra to survive. Our education never suffered. We were hardly off school. Our parents were not lazy. Our parents never encouraged any one of us to sleep in, that's for old people. As for new skills, what means did we have to afford the items that would give you better skills, like reading, ie books, like hobbies, ie cycling, archery, board games. They all cost money. Even sports activities, darts, cricket, rugby, tennis, all cost money.

As for being more academic, again the answer is no. We were blessed with great genes and none of us were going to be Philadelphia lawyers. But then again, none of us were going to starve. Why? Because we were blessed with the Booth Warburton genes which in two words means not lazy.

S I believe we took in every skill we learnt as four boys growing up in Liverpool 5. The street to us was a daily challenge and it was our back yard. We worked, we learnt and we developed. That is as good as it gets. It was a journey of 7, 8 9, 10-year-old babies going off into the world using your brains, your energy, to make things to work for you together as four boys. Today you are called entrepreneurs. Come on, beat that.

And my answer to them questions would be no.

The alternative would be terminal sit in the house all day, in a two up two down terrace where you could not swing a cat, go to our room and study or play games. Sorry all we had our room was a bed and the four lads. Two up tow down, with a gob full of feet in your mouth every night. Not very exciting. No computer, no laptops, no iPad, no games, no phones, no central heating, no telly. Weren't we lucky. You decide. That's the alternative.

Our paths have taken us on great journeys. We have all embraced far more than our parents who deserved to have it all but it was a sign of the times and our parents put themselves on the line to feed, look after and bring us up. That's how it was. They could not and would not have looked any further than that. Were we any different? No. Street in street out were all doing the same. Answer: born at the wrong time.

But their kids will thrive and prosper and multiply. And we did in a big way. The Lord said come forth and multiply and we almost broke the mould. The Boothies that is.

Chapter 4 – Hopes and Fears, and Future Years

When we all eventually grew up and went out in the big world, I am sure we all had great hopes. None of us, I am sure, had only aspirations of becoming a Philadelphia lawyer to coin a phrase. But amidst the fears of finding the right path to go down, we all tried to navigate our lives, not always in the way we thought. However, whatever the outcome we all more or less, except for our John, came through unscathed.

We have to start with the youngest of the four, our Ray. As I have said in the book, he came into the business late. I think he was 7, but I was sure in later years he would excel in anything you put before him. He was a model pupil. He left school and went right into work and started to climb the ladder.

As well as being a grafter he had the Boothie head on him. He started as a tyre fitter in Derning Road, then mechanic. His next move was to Huyton Volkswagon in Wilson Road. He was first tools, then service, visor MOT instructor etc. This was his formative working years after that brain kicked in. And he became his own man. Without going into great detail, he became a very successful business man. He never took prisoners.

He was a great example of what can be achieved if you apply yourself through work, drive, knowledge and ambition. He had all them qualities as his oldest brother.

I had always known he would make something of his life, it goes back to when we were kids, having to take orders from me for years. He probably said, wait and see, one day I will be the delegator. It came to pass for a Boothie.

Then there was our Alan. He had a lot of good qualities as a boy. He had energy, the looks, the height and the strength. As kids I would play with the idea when sending both Alan and John out to sell the firewood, that I could have made our Alan carry 24 bundles rather than 12. But he wouldn't have it. I wasn't going to argue with him. Our John was on his side. They all hated me because I was a slave driver. I was.

I was called some names and you know what, I was bad. A little bit of power and it worked. Try doing that today. No chance. Alan had a few jobs, they all entailed heavy work in factories, on the building, for British Rail. All long hours and hard work. He had to, he had a big family to support – 7 in all. I call then the magnificent seven. All tall, all beautiful and good looking. Of course, they have 50% Boothie blood. So, with Alan and Sue's two boys, Alan, Steven, the Boothie brand carries on.

They will never have to do what we done. But I wonder if it worked for us. But what else was there? Our Alan was and is a big person was a part of the Boothie treadmill. He was a hard worker and a sound brother. He and Sue have performed miracles bringing up the children. All the girls have really excelled in all manner of jobs and now most of them are high up in the NHS. Not only is Alan and Sue proud of them and the boys, but we as a family are. And their grandkids are awesome. Gentlemen and ladies though and through. Are you already our Alan?

Dad and Mam at a family party

Now John, the Bogie, our Alan's mate, the quiet man so they said. When he gave you that look your impression would change. He had the looks of a choir boy but fists as hard and as fast as a cheetah. If looks could kill. If he said 'move it' you went quickly. John was a hard worker. He never deserved his fate. I am sure if he had married with kids he would be still here. Its only opinion. He was a great barman. Worked all hours but he was soft. He gave to everyone and some turned Judas. He was no problem unless you got wrong side of him and the look alone would scare you off. I was never as close to John as Alan was. They were real mates. They drank together, worked together and fought together. Our John was quick, Alan was hard. If he connected you have gone. What a combination 'The Mighty Atom' and the 'Draught Champ'. You never messed with them but they were young then.

We were new to the area then when we arrived in Walton. We four were teenagers, 13 up. I was at sea when we moved from Gordon Street. John and Alan continued to look after each other. John was well sought after. He would run the pubs while the licensees were on holiday and he could run them. He was fast and nippy at work. He helped hundreds and dozens let him down. He was an easy tough. But when he died at 49 you could not get in the church he was that popular.

We all loved the Bogie. He will always be the best cellar man, barman, Walton will ever have.

Then there was me. John, Alan and Ray were right. I was a slave driver, a bully, and a big headed get, and not much has changed. I was cunning, cock sure, but it all worked. We got results. We were top dogs. We were copied in everything we done because we were a team. We were all out for the same end results – money. And who got the bulk of it? Not me, not my brothers, but my mam.

She was the only reason we carried on with those various pursuits purely because we had respect for our parents. We wanted to help. There was no one like our mam. She gave us everything. We never wanted for anything. We were well fed, always clean and tidy. She was a one off. Since them days, over 55 years ago, we have come a long way. Our parents gave us faith and made us proud and with their genes you had a head start.

I started my working life, I mean my official working life, at Venmore Contractors at 15 years of age at that point. I had already worked seven years as a boy. Venmores was hard work and little pay but I gathered the knowledge.

My workmates were great. Jimmy Gibbo, Ned, Charlie Stitchcome, Alan Bellogamba, Mr Harris, Mr Foy, Jimmy George. Billy Walker was my work mate and I kept in touch with him and his family. I loved Billy. Kenny, his son, played for Liverpool and his wife worked in the local car sales. Billy's wife – not Kenny's. His wife was a friend of ours. In my youth, I went out with her sister – a great family. I miss Bill Walker 'who's home on the range'.

From Venmores, at not yet 16, I was off to Sharpness, Gloucester, to do my sea training. Remember, I am only a boy but going away from home for eight weeks to a strange part of the country for someone who has never left Liverpool. Could today's kids do it? Remember, there were no mobile phones, not being able to see and talk to parents and friends. Today's kids are still at school at 15.

We were up at 5.30 sharp, on the parade ground at 6 o'clock. Imagine that. It was winter when I arrived, it was freezing in only shorts and best. After we would wash, dressed and then down to the quay. And then we would board the Vindicatrix ('Vindi' for short) for breakfast. And what a breakfast! The porridge never left the pan. The bacon and eggs were cardboard and the beans looked as though they had been regurgitated. The toast was passable but the tea, God knows. It was not drinkable. Anyway, after that hearty breakfast work began on board ship where the classrooms were.

In the evening we would go to the mess room and play darts and some indoor sports. At weekends we would go into Berkley to the cinema. Time went slow. It was very quiet out there as time passed. We had life boat drill on the River Severn, learnt seamanship and our chosen career was catering which we done day in day out. How to present and serve tables, cooking skills etc. We were given a test. God help you if you failed after being away that long from home.

We were not free students. Our parents paid. My dad was then a docker and my mother a cleaner. They were not rich but that was what I wanted to do and they helped me by paying for my training. I had to pass out. If you failed there was no second chance. I was home and your seafaring days finished. My dad went to sea, my Grandad, so I had to go. Anyway, the test took two hours. There was forty in our class. You had to get a high score in order to pass. I came third out of forty boys. I couldn't believe it. Me, Boothie from Greaty, all ready for sea.

After a few days we were going home. I felt six foot instead of five foot nothing. I boarded the train, next stop Lime Street. I had on my Vindi uniform, my hat, kit bag over my shoulder. I thought I was the business. My brothers saw me and started laughing. Who cares? I felt good.

A week or so later a taxi pulled up outside. My mam said, "It's for your Billy". It was the Chief Steward and Second Steward. The taxi took off for the docks. We went aboard, I signed on. I was given a cabin. Now I was a seaman – still only 15 years old.

The ship was called the MV Malatian. She was the sister ship to the Maltasian and the company was Ellerman Pappyani. We were off, first port of all Piraeus, Greece. I was a commi-cook/pantry boy.

We were scheduled to be away six to eight weeks. Again, today's kids couldn't be away from home for two days without crying for their home comforts or where my phone or my crutches. Not the Boothies, we were right in there 'One Life'.

I was up at 5.30 each morning and cleaned my cabin then turned to the first three days I spent more time being sick, bent over a sink in the galley. I had to carry on working, either strapped to the sink cleaning dishes and pans. I then had to assist Benni, the steward, with the officers' breakfast. Then when breakfast was over I had to clean the officers' cabins. Once all that was done I had my breakfast then prepare lunch, peel spuds, prepare veg, then assist Benni in the saloon for lunch. Same routine, prepare tea, etc. Between six and seven in the evening, a few free hours in the mess, then ready for bed. The next day another 12-hour shift.

Remember this was every day you were at sea, not in port. But you still had your duties before you could go ashore.

Arriving in Piraeus, imagine the first country I had ever been to, and just 16. I was the only boy on board. All the others were men. I was escorted with them, a few bars, a brothel, but I was a boy, young naïve, I got through the night. Enough said.

The place was amazing, but you know what when you're young, you don't appreciate it. Time flies. From there were went to Beirut, Lattakia, then Famagusta, Cyprus, then Alexandria, Egypt. Them places opened your eyes to the world out there. In Alexandria the dockers lived on the dock. Its another world. Next stop Dublin, then home. So, before I was 16 and a quarter I had been to Greece, to five different countries. The weather was good on our return journey. I sat on deck peeled spuds. It was only a small ship, 20 crew. On our arrival I signed on again for Portugal and the Jewish run.

When I got home my dad was on the quay. I had to go through customs and get paid off, but my dad and tony went aboard, they were dockers, so they could. My dad got some players, some whiskey, some money and he was off.

I got a taxi home and I felt like a man, well not quite. I was soon brought back to earth by my dad's mates when I went to the pub with him.

Remember, I am 16, No 1 son, in a pub in Liverpool. Abroad no one cares. Here I am 16, I managed to down a few bottles of Guinness then I got off.

I enjoyed my time on the Malatian. My mate John Kenny looked after me on my first trip. He had just returned. He was about 10 years older than me but he came from the same area. He was a good laugh and we were mates after a few more trips with Malatian then I was off to pastures new.

I went to Shell next. I was on the SS Hinea, all Indian crew bar catering and officers. I was away five months and it went everywhere.

After my Shell experience I was next with Harrisons on the Custodian Plainsman and Astronomer, all over West Africa, Durban Freetown, Port Elizabeth, etc.

Then back to Shell, around the Gulf, all the Arab ports. After that it was Empress of Canada, and the QE2.

I joined the Empress of Canada because my mate I met at the Vindi sea school had also signed on. He was a bell boy or bell hop. I was in the galley. It was a big ship. I was used to the long hours. We would turn to have various jobs before we went into the Galley. We would clean all the windows, doors, alleyways in the passenger accommodation rea, the bulkheads, saloon glass, doors, etc, then washed, into the galley and start catering for 1-2,000 bloods, we called the passengers.

Today all that pre-work before galley duty is done by various staff. It was long hours, hard work, 15-16-hour days from 5.30 to 7-8.30, but we were young and once finished we would hit the bar for a few bevvies.

The steward would knock us up. There were at least eight in a cabin, mostly galley and saloon staff. Once we had done our duties, breakfast could consist of anything, poached eggs, steak, gammon, salmon. The food was top drawer.

There would be two sittings for breakfast, lunch and dinner. The waiters (or wingers as they were known) would be rushed off their feet, back and forth to the galley for at least 14 days, with stops at Montreal and Quebec for a 17-day trip, three trip articles.

The wingers got great tips. For two weeks they could end up with 100-200 dollars each. We were on £34 per month, so that's real cash. They would all go ashore and do the bars and we 'junior ratings' would go to the cinema. Three shows for a buck – 1 dollar.

It was in Montreal where I got my one and only tattoo. We were all pissed so we all went. Me being wise got a bird with mam and dad on it. I knew my mam would blow up. And she did. I showed her it was them on my arm, you do thinks like that when you're young, it's called rebel.

Anyway, from Montreal we set sail to Quebec. It's so arty there, very Lark Lane, nothing but artists, paintings, mostly French speaking quarter. There is a set of steps up to the village from the quay. I tell you, you have to be fit. We were kids, at least 200 steps, but what a view from the top.

The Canada was a great ship and I done a few trips then went cruising with her from New York to West Indies, Jamaica, Happy Valley, etc. They were the days. We done the lot, I mean the lot. By the time I was 18 I had been to 50 countries. Today most 18-year olds, well not all, have not had a job, are still in bed till lunchtime and when they do get a job, they do the same job for 30 to 50 years. Come on get a life, same old same old.

Anyway, life on board them passenger liners were great. There must have been 50 lads in catering all between 16 and 18 years old. We had a ball. If we were not working we would be bronzing the days away. We had the world at our feet. They were very long hours, not your 9 to 5 drab existence. When you're young you live life to the full before the ball and chain gets attached. Come on, they were 15-hour days. You finished, went to the Pig, sunk a few pints, played some cards or roulette with flash some darts, then bed at 12 o'clock and up at 5 o'clock. You can always tell a seaman, ex or otherwise, how they apply themselves, the way they set things out. Just setting out a buffet, the way they glaze the salmon, pig etc. It's the way they were trained. All the best cooks, roast sauce fish pastry bakers etc, it's nautical, you can tell, a gift trained by the best, by Gods, if you like. There was Blackie the head chef, the Dutchman extra chef, Little Jimmy, he was from around my territory, Scottie Road. He drank in the Holy House. They were cooks. Blackie was great with all the commi cooks. He got me on raw eggs and mackerel and we had a choice of anything. But he said the Bombay oysters will look after your guts, and the mackerel will look after your heart and brain. He never mentioned your liver, purely by that time most seamen had a drink problem.

Who knows how things turn out, you get on with it. One life, I never ever seen Blackie again. I believe he lived on the Wirral. The Dutchman I saw, he opened a chippy in Litherland by the Salt Box Pub and Jimmy I saw a lot in the Holy House, drinking with my dad and Tony Bennett.

Most of the lads I sailed with on the Canada were from around Scotty. They were Robbie Barnes, Tony Delahunty, Eddie McCame, Ingy and Omo from the buildings. Scottie and Vauxhall was a big merchant seaman's area. I kept in touch with a lot of the lads as me and my dad drank down Scottie regular and my brothers, Tony Bennett, Billy Wignall, Georgie Connor, Cisco, Paddy Bennett all my dad's mates, mostly dockers, sadly Scotty went the same way as the pubs, and along with Scottie, the characters died too.

One by one they went, along with our dad, all gone never to return. It was a privilege to live there, laugh there, and to be around young at that time in the sixties, with no political correctness, no health and safety. Live and let live days. When no one had anything yet had time for each other, not like today when people are more interested in what other people are doing with their lives than what they're doing with their own lives "Facebook". One day they will turn around and say, 'I'm 64, what have I don with my life?'. The same old, same old. Nothing.

So, after Canadian Pacific, working by and around the coast work, I called it a day. I met my future wife, Cathy, and settled down with kids. But as a young boy I ad been everywhere, done everything. What 15-21-year-old can say that today, 1-1000 or more the odds will get longer. Some might work 5-10 years in their lifetime. Some may wait for the saga years to come along so they can do less and say I am over 50, so what.

Cath and me both at 20 years old.

My wife, Cathy, is unique with what she has done in one lifetime most women could not fit into ten. She's an institution in Garston. She left school at 15 having already worked in her uncle's chandlery shop since she was 11. She went to hairdressing college in Colquitt Street and trained in top salons in Liverpool and West Derby. She opened her own salon in 1969 and it's still there to this day as I write this book, 50 years in business in 2019!

Me and Cath, Wedding Day, aged 21 and 22 in 1970

She has brought literally hundreds of young people into the workplace, been a member of the Guild of Hairdressers, Chairwoman of Notre Dame High School in Woolton. She's had over a dozen other businesses and had time to have three daughters while still working 60-70 hours a week.

We only had our first continental holiday together when we celebrated our 25th wedding anniversary. And she's still working! How many women do you know with that CV, done over 30 years charity work, gets up happy, laughs and smiles all day, goes home happy, is not always well but never complains. But look, she is an employer not an employee. She is not supposed to be happy. She takes it with a pinch of salt. Why?

Because she comes from intelligent, hard working stock, gifted, talented all excelled in their field. She is extraordinary and what she has done in her lifetime, she has no peers. It proves that with one life you can leave a legacy.

She has helped to train, educate and give something back. It would never have been done if I had married a couch potato more interested in what other people do. Her life has been purposeful, rich and rewarding and I am proud of her along with her community help, charity work and Buckingham Palace invite. Her journey has been rich. There can't be many out there with a CV to match that (Jeremy Kyle next, not likely).

Cathy

Chapter 5 – Bucket List and Ambitions

Having started my working life at Venmores in Venice Street, Anfield as an apprentice plumber and stayed eight months. From there to Sharpness, Gloucester for sea training school MV Vindicatrix for eight weeks as a 15-year-old. Then into the Merchant Navy and worked for six shipping companies. I travelled all over the world by the time I was 21.

Then I got married and took at job on the buses as a conductor. I worked in the mortuary and on the site of John Bagot Hospital as a porter. Then I worked on building sites as a hod carrier and labourer. I then had a succession of jobs, shipping butchers Grossfields, Bibbys, Land & Watt Bonded Warehouse, Grown Restaurant. Then more building, Lester Joinery, Ritson McKenzie. Then on the Wirral, Tan Yard, Birkenhead, The Adelphi, etc, after all that knowledge, I said to Cathy, train me to be a hairdresser. She trained me for five years.

After that I opened a newsagents in Wallasey. From there I had a meat delivery business, then a large window cleaning round in Thornton.

No time for breath, I started to open a chain of hair salons in north Liverpool called "Faces".

After running that company for 10 years I then did some work with Group 4 Security. After that, onto Securicor. After working 10 years for the security firms I felt like a change.

We relocated our original business, ie Cathy's of Garston, which by then had traded for 27 years under the bridge in Garson. We moved half a mile down the road into the Village to larger premises that could house three businesses with flats above.

Our journey wasn't yet complete. We moved from Garston to Melling in 1984 and along with Robbie Corrie we managed to start three boys' football teams in the village which were very successful. We managed to win numerous trophies with the help and assistance of Olive Mason and Alan Brown off the Melling Parish Council who funded and encouraged activities in the village. With their help we were able to implement continuous football for boys age range 8-14. That period of my life was satisfying because the village had been without any form of boys' football so it was very pleasing Robbie and myself were successful for 14 years. We move on.

In the interim, me and Cathy started our charity work which we have done now for 34 years. We have worked with Marcia Hughes who ran the

BBC Charitable Trust. I have met hundreds of celebs, watched the rise of Rachel Russell from a young girl develop into one of the top opera singers in the world. WE have met some very unassuming people during our charity duties. We are very fond of Roger Phillips of BBC Radio Merseyside as our business has for nearly 50 years traded in south Liverpool so Roger has done boundless work there and is a great ambassador for south Liverpool.

This is my third book of a trilogy about the Booth family and my previous work and royalties have been passed to the charities me and Cath have been lucky to have been nominated by the people of south Liverpool, hence our visit to the Buckingham Palace Garden Party. While staying at the Rubens on the Mall and taking in the Ritz, etc.

Two of our three children have been university educated, currently sitting their masters, while the third is very successful in her own field.

We are still working 50 hours a week, are now close to 70 as I write this book, have three daughters, six grandchildren, four girls, two boys, one boy even named after me. Not bad for a 15-year-old who had just left Rossi and thought where do I go from here. Come on, follow that CV.

Having achieved that in one lifetime I am still hopeful that God spares me to go on and achieve other goals. The bucket list is not complete. As I write this book I am only 70. What can I do now? Any suggestions? Please save me from daytime telly! Me and Cath are still running our companies, Cathy's of Garston will be 50 years trading on 9 August 2019. And Jermaines One will have been trading for 21 years also in 2019. God spares us, we will retire then, we will see.

The Boothies, all four of us, have had full lives, except for our John who died young. But what he achieved in them forty-nine years most people could not fit in one hundred.

Alan and Ray have also had full lives. Ray is a successful businessman and travelled the world. They have two academically successful children in Neil and Rachel.

Alan, along with Sue, has a lovely family. All the children are firstly models and then beautiful, including Alan and Steven. I am extremely proud of Jacqueline and Mike, their children, stand out in a crowd. And I am sure for all of them the world is their oyster.

I am sure the NHS are pleased and proud to have Boothie genes working for them as me and Cath are proud too.

I am sure Alan and Sue are proud as punch all their children and grandchildren are a credit to them. Another Boothie success story.

I remember all of Alan and Sue's children, my nieces and nephews, sitting on the couch or running around the living room with runny noses, all babies and I would watch their faces light up when I brought them sweets. Now look at them, I need a ladder these days.

I do feel that as four young boys we were fortunate to have the platform, experience and brotherly love we had as kids to come through them early years. What a tool to go forward. In later life you had to be good to kid the Booths. There wasn't many our equal. We had the Boothie stamp. We were fit, clever, wary and wise. We used all them skills in life and as you have read in the book, the boys done good.

The remaining years we have ahead of us we would like to visit as many places as possible. We have already navigated ourselves all over Scotland and the Highlands, Jersey and the Channel Islands, the Isle of Man, been on 10 cruise holidays and travelled most of the United Kingdom. WE have travelled all over Europe and know Spain and Italy intimately.

But we have not yet discovered Ireland so like most of the Holy Shrine pilgrimages we have been on. I am sure Ireland has one or two there, so the journey is not over.

I hope to write more books, not family based, more to do with observation, findings and thoughts of what we have seen together. I hope my mam and dad and John are looking down on us all and saying, you now what, Bill, John, the lads have done well and we done them proud. And I would like to thank my mam and dad for the opportunity to give something back, when you think of what we nicked as kids. Only joking!

I want to thank all them people, institutions, schools, boys' clubs, etc who have moulded the Boothies into the adults they have become. The people like Mr Meek, my English Teacher in Penrhyn Street. He was strict but he was the man who taught me to love English literature to improve my spelling. He gave me confidence at seven, my lucky number.

All the customers who gave us the opportunity to improve our entrepreneurial skills and learn from the good and bad pay days we had. Mr Packenham (Paki) for encouraging us to set a precedent to find out what we could do and how far we could go.

None of us had a vision, we just lived from day to day, like everyone it was a mundane life. But without those entrepreneurial adventures, without them reasons to get up in the morning, what would we have had to look back on? I would not have achieved enough to write a trilogy of books on our youth. All the kids we knew went from birth to teenagers then the real world. We had already served our apprenticeship. The way we bonded as kids is totally different to the way siblings bond today because we grew not only as four then five brothers, as young entrepreneurs. But our whole being developed from our business brain, energy levels, that we have taken with us from boys into our adult life.

It gave us a head start. We had already been there, had nothing to prove, we had in fact served our time, yet we were still teenagers. It was all locked away, stored upstairs, ready for release.

We have worked all our lives, no benefits, passed it onto our kids who are doing the same. No relying on something to wake you up and something to put you to sleep, it's called genes. But without the energy, adrenalin and will to reach your goal, objective, call it what you like, you will not make it. When you have been in business for 49 years in this jungle and are still out there then you have cracked it.

The Boothies have been on a remarkable journey. I never thought we would all come out intact, but we did. Our young lives was always balanced on a knife edge. In them early days when we were stripping roofs of its lead, taking windows out to be sold on, stripping copper wires from floorboards, all the houses were condemned, they were all of skeleton proportions all ready to collapse because they had all been stripped to their bare minimum. Today's health and safety laws would not have stood a chance in them days. Why? Because kids them days were instinctive, inventive and brave. The words political correctness were not even heard of, thank God. What a world it would have been.

I am sure all my brothers would agree our time as kids were the best and we were lucky to be born when kids could be kids. Inventive, happy, carefree. Not like today when you can't move or play safely in the streets and even 10 years olds are carrying mobile phones.

The Boothies have been there, done that, worn the t-shirt and sold the s-shirt on. Typical Boothies. Entrepreneurs to the end.

The Boothies were made up of six children, five boys and one girl. I have not deliberately set out to exclude Wayne and Gail from the story, but the book is centred on four boys, all one year apart. Wayne and Gail came along nine/10 years later then the Boothies had already become folklore. Wayne, my youngest brother, would have been a massive asset had he arrived one year after Ray. Why? Because he was tall, good looking, a great footballer, he would have been ideal when we were pinching clothes off the washing lines to weight in as rags. Because of his height no need to be bunged up. Only kidding!

Wayne and Mary have worked all their lives. Wayne currently has been with the GPO nearly 40 years. Mary has a responsible job in the city, they have three very beautiful and talented children, Kevin, Sarah and Maria, and not forgetting Billybob, my namesake. All of our Wayne's many talents would have took us to greater heights but fortunately for him, he never had to go out in the cold, take orders from me and anyway, if he was round then, he would be drawing his state pension by now.

Then the last Boothie was a girl, my mam and dad's saviour. Gail never had to go through any of them chores, go out in the dark, or do any dirty work. Why? Because she was a girl and the youngest. Gail married to Brian has a daughter Clare, and two grandchildren Poppy and Frankie. Clare is married to Kev. Gail worked for Boots for many years and ended up working as a beauty consultant for Rimmel when ill health retired her. Brian has worked in the building industry all his life. They live in Walton and thankfully are looking after are parents' last home where they were happy.. Clare and Kevin worked for Liverpool City Council and Kevin still works there. Clare is bringing up the children, one has even inherited my mother's name. I am sure Gail turned out to be a girl, number six Boothie, purely because she would have had to take orders from me, God forbid.

Catherine Warburton and Jane Booth, nee Warburton

Chapter 6 - The Chalice or F.A. Cup

When we were kids we would often play football tournaments at weekends. Whoever got to the final would play for the cup or chalice.

If we never won the final and we lost the cup then we would have to arrange another tournament in order to win back the cup or chalice. Why? Well, the chalice belonged to my dad, and it took pride of place in my mam's china cabinet in the living room.

Now we don't know how our dad came across the chalice. Did he pick it up somewhere when he was out with the barra, tatting, or was it given to him? Did he win it playing darts? I doubt it. Okay, would our dad have robbed it from a church? It would never have crossed my dad's mind to do that!

But my dad relied on that cup or chalice being in the china cabinet, so if he was skint, he would pawn it for a few pints.

The moral of this story is: we must have all been great footballers because the cup still belongs to the Boothies sixty years later!

Me and Cath at Peter Collings 50 years in business

Cath and me and our horse, Jasuka

Cath and Bill at a family wedding

Bill and Cath at Jane's house in Aughton

Melling Boys managed by Bill and Robbie

Jermaines sponsored football team. Jermaine Mascot 2000

Centre forward midfielder mascot

Girl power . . . the seven year old proving to be a lucky mascot

● Table toppers . . . Jermaines are currently flying high at the top of the Skelmersdale League first division. The team is pictured with sponsor Mr W Booth and the team mascot, his granddaughter Jermaine. Mr Booth named the team after his seven year-old grandchild, who lives in Ormskirk. Jermaine also gave her name to his South Liverpool company, Jermaines Health, Fitness and Beauty, which sponsors the team.

Jane with Will and Reuben at graduation

My beautiful daughter, Suzie, at sweet sixteen

Will, my namesake, me and Evie, when they were young

Some of the gifts and hampers to be donated to Zoe's Place, KIND and the League of Welldoers. Thank you to all who donated.

Afternoon tea at Ritz Hotel, London
The day after our Garden Party invite at Buckingham Palace.

ECHO

News / Scouse Proud

There's so much for us to be proud of here

SCOUSE PROUD

PADDY SHENNAN MEETS A COUPLE WHO HAVE PUT COMMUNITY FIRST

Answers to Quiz in Book 2

If you have not read Book 2, you will not know the questions. So, get Book 2 now.

1. The Spot

2. Leo's

3. Whites Cazeneu Street end, Lever and Martins, Boundary Street end

4. The Duffy's. A goal business/a sweet shop a public house

5. Paddy Donnelly

6. Jacksons, brother and sister

7. The Oporto

8. Bottom of Everton Brow

9. He was instrumental in funding the building of Penrhyn Street School and further education, bottom of Gordon Street.

10. Pickles, by putting your coin in the slot machine if it went around and never dropped through you won a woody (a woodbine, The Great Little Cigarette) happy days.

How many did you get?

If you got 10, a real Greaty-ite. Well done.

If you got 7, not much escaped you.

If you got 4, getting to know the area.

If you got none, should have got out more.

Quiz

These questions will be answered when I write Book 4, entitled 'Back In The Day'

1.   Where did the famous Greaty Echo Seller liver?

2.   What was his nickname?

3.   What shop did two sisters own?

4.   Where was it?

5.   Name the chippy hallway up Conway Street.

6.   Name the chippy bottom of Elias Street.

7.   Name the woodyard half way up Elias Street.

8.   Name the famous footballer who lived in Penrhyn Street.

9.   Name the Bents Pub, bottom of Bostock Street – Bossi

10.   Name the sweet shop by the entry, bottom of Gordon Street

11.   Name the Bents Pub, facing the Farmers Arms, Roscommon Street

12.   Name the pub bottom of Jason Street

13.   Name the street were Reeces Milk was

14.   Name chippy next to wine store, facing Robsart Street

15.   What shop sold various teas and broken biscuits

16.   Name the grocers, bottom of Newsham Place

17.   Name shop bottom of Bostock Street

18.   What was the name of the butcher's shop facing Conway Castle

19.   Where did Paddy Donnelly live, the commissionaire of Homer Cinema?

20.   Name the tramp who walked Greaty week in week out.

The Boothies
She Laughed More than She Cried

As four we worked together

We formed a real good bond

No-one else could match us

Together we were strong

We were up before the dawn

And out and on the streets

While everyone was sleeping

The Boothies bagged their treats

They never knew what hit hem

They really were that good

We tried to be so crafty

As anybody would

We were only children

Trying to do good

Searching in the jungle

For rags, metal and wood

We tried to help many people

Yes, we thought we done good

We came, we took, we delivered

Like your proverbial Robin Hood

The Boothies (circa 1956-1965)

Charities helped by Cathy's & Jermaine's One from 1969 to 2019

Zoe's Place

K.I.N.D.

James Bulger Appeal

Air Ambulance Service

Royal National Lifeboat Institution

Garston, Speke Sea Cadets

Broadgreen Radio

League of Welldoers

Accord Hospice, Paisley

Roya Castle Foundation

Garston Day Nursery

Banks Road School

Holy Trinity School

Jet South Liverpool

Charities to benefit from Bill's latest books

Liverpool 5: Book 2

The Boothies: Book 3

Zoe's Place

K.I.N.D.

League of Welldoers

Charities to benefit from book 4

Shrewsbury Boy's Club

Carla Lane Animal Sanctuary, Melling

Afterword

It has given me great pleasure writing this trilogy of books. I have drawn on my memory and a small amount of research. A friend, Dougie Mannering provided me with some of the photos, while a few I had stored away. My boyhood memories keep flooding back. I have always been able to draw on my memory which is a gift passed on by my Nanny Kate Warburton. A mine of information my nan was. I have come to the end of Book 3. I hope it brings back memories to all that read it. Book1 and Book2 are also available. The charities that will benefit from sales of the books:

Zoes Place, children under 5, West Derby

KIND, a wonderful children's charity run by an amazing man, Stephen Yip and his staff

I would also like to mention the **League of Welldoers** in Limekiln Lane off Scotland Road, one of the oldest charities in Liverpool. They have done a wonderful job in helping to stave off poverty for generations of people in the Vauxhall area for over a century since Mr Lee Jones founded it. We will make a donation to this charity.

We have recently added The Shrewsbury Boys Club and the Melling Animal Sanctuary to our list for donations in 2020-2021.

Apologies

My apologies go to Billy Lambert. I cannot exclude one of the eleven picked for the Great Neddy Eleven but Billy Lambert should have been one of my first out. Sorry Billy!

I mentioned in Book One that our woodwork teacher was Mr Chisnal. I was wrong. It was Mr Martinson. This was pointed out to me by an old friend, ex-schoolmate and ex-Vindi Boy, John Edwards of Beatrice Street. Thank you, John.

W H Booth Jnr

Printed in Great Britain
by Amazon